Harri Kuisti

Rubik's Cube
Only 3+4 Moves
to Remember

Kustantaja: BoD – Books on Demand, Helsinki, Suomi

Valmistaja: BoD – Books on Demand, Norderstedt, Saksa

ISBN: 978-952-80-7025-2

Can you count your fingers?
Congratulations!
Solving the cube is easy for you.

Do you need memory capacity or brain power?

Solving the Rubik's cube is sometimes seen either as an intellectual feat or as a challenge to your memory. Both of these notions are far from reality. I truly respect mathematicians that are able to turn the cube into a fascinating excercise of group theory. I am sure they are right but you do not need to think like them in order to solve the cube.

Many on the other hand have made it all a matter of speed. Solving the cube fast is not possible without memorizing a large number of series of moves or algorithms as they are called.

This book shows a third way: Understanding the cube in simple terms and reducing the solution to tiny bits. You do not need to strain your brain or memory to any large extent. Can you count your fingers? Then you are fit to the simple task of solving the Rubik' cube.

Standard moves

First some basic information: The Left-, Right-hand side, Upside, Downside, Front or Back layers are turned in clockwise direction with moves called L, R, U, D, F and B. The counter-clockwise turns are marked by l', r', u', d', f' and b'.

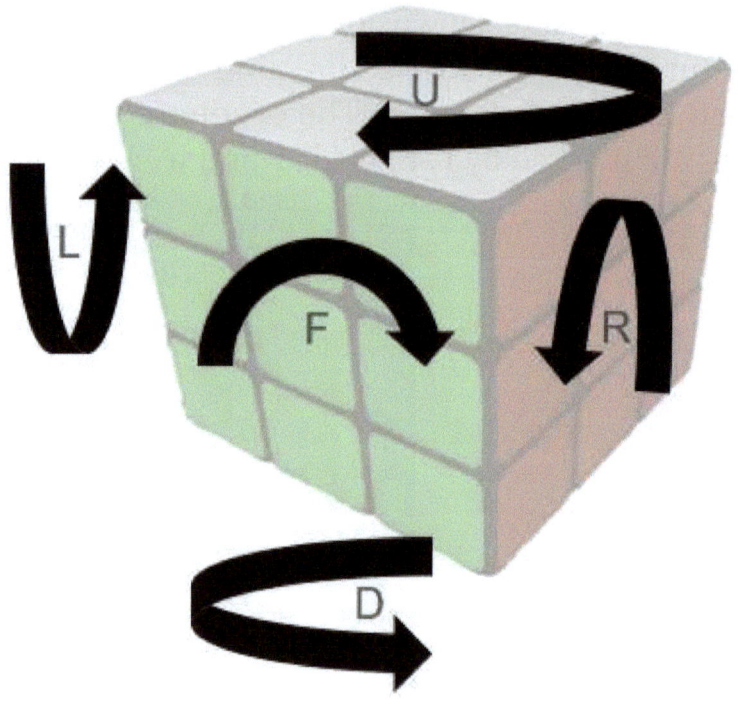

Figure 1. Different clockwise moves of the Rubik's cube. The one turning the backside (B) facet or plane clockwise (B) is not shown.

Table 1. The naming of the moves.

	Clockwise	Counter-clockwise
Left hand -side plane	L	l'
Right hand -side plane	R	r'
Frontside plane	F	f'
Backside plane	B	b'
Upside plane	U	u'
Downside plane	D	d'

The phases of the solution

The famous Beginner's Solution is based on solving the cube layer by layer. The method presented in this book solves the edges first and then the corners. This is no new idea as such. The new thing (as far as I know) is that only one algorithm of three moves is needed for placing and orienting the edges correctly, and just one algorithm of four moves is needed for doing the same for corners.

I will soon show those elementary series of moves. At this stage it is enough to say that the process has two phases:

1) Solving edges
2) Solving corners

Solving the edges can be divided into separate stages:

1) Creating the white cross.
2) Solving the edges of the sides.
3) Creating the yellows cross.
4) Placing the pieces of the yellow cross correctly.

Also solving the corners can be divided into separate stages:

1) Placing the corners of the layer with white center piece.
2) Placing the corners of the layer with yellow center piece.
3) Orienting the corners.

Creating the white cross

Almost all methods invented for solving the Rubik's cube begin with creating a white cross. This means turning all planes so that on the plane that have a white middle piece there appear white colour on all edges. It does not matter if there are even more white pieces around the cross. We do not need to care about that in this phase.

Figure 2. Examples of "white cross". The colours around the white cross can be whatever, and it does not matter. This is illustrated by the rightmost pattern where the grey stands for "any colour".

You can easily create a cross of any colour, as you will see if you just turn the planes for fun. There is nothing difficult in this phase and nothing to memorize. The cube itself will guide you in this.

There is however one additional requirement for a white cross and that concerns the colours of the other planes or facets: The colour of the middle pieces on all sizes has to be the same as that of the edge piece forming a part of the white cross.

Figure 3. Examples of side plane colours when there is a "white cross" on the plane with white middle piece. The colours around the edge piece and the middle piece can be whatever, and it does not matter. This is illustrated by the bottom row representing patterns where the grey stands for "any colour".

Three magic moves

The three moves are easy to learn. You can see and understand what happens when applying them, so there is less need to memorize them. It is a matter of taste whether the three simple moves deserve to be called an algorithm at all and if we want see the right- and left-hand side versions as different, because they are basically identical, being only mirroring series of moves.

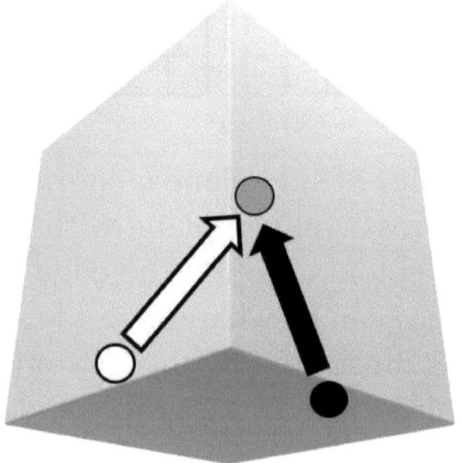

Figure 5. The transition repeated many times when placing and orienting the edges. The transitions depicted by white and black arrows are basically identical involving just three moves.

The following figures illustrate placing of the edge pieces of the side planes into their correct positions. There are four edge pieces to be placed at this stage but there are two possible initial orientations for each, which result in eight different cases. They are however basically identical.

It is easy to find the edge pieces to be brought into their places and to move them to the initial positions given in the figures.

In the figure 6 one example of using the three basic moves for changing the position and orientation of edge pieces.

Figure 6. An example of moving edge pieces. Note that two of pieces are marked with letters in order to make it easier to see how the pieces move (obviously the whole plane rotates as well).

It has been explained previously that the three moves used for edges are in essence identical and mirroring each other. This can be easily seen by comparing the figures 6 and 7.

Figure 7. An example of replacement piece coming from the opposite direction than in figure 6.

If you wish you can use the naming of Table 1 at page 7 and say that bringing the midlayer corner pieces into correct locations utilizes the following series of moves:

r'DR (the correct edge piece coming from the left)

Ld'l' (the correct edge piece coming from the right)

Note that what can be called left and right obviously depends on how you hold the cube. Regardless that the way the pieces move is rather easy to perceive.

Creating the yellow cross

In this method the creation of the yellow cross follows the same ideas as when putting the edge pieces in their correct places. We just use the same easy-to-understand moves as before.

When the edges of the top-most white plane and the side edges are in correct positions this means that the edges of the yellow plane are already somewhere on that plane. But it is likely that they need help in finding their correct places and orientations. We start by orienting them so that their yellow sides point in the same and correct direction.

We already placed the edge pieces correctly but now we must temporarily disturb that order. Sorry for that! But it will soon be all good again.

First we rotate the bottom layer in such a way that as many as possible edges are correct as to their location and orientation. After that we repeat the transitions explained previously until the yellow cross appears.

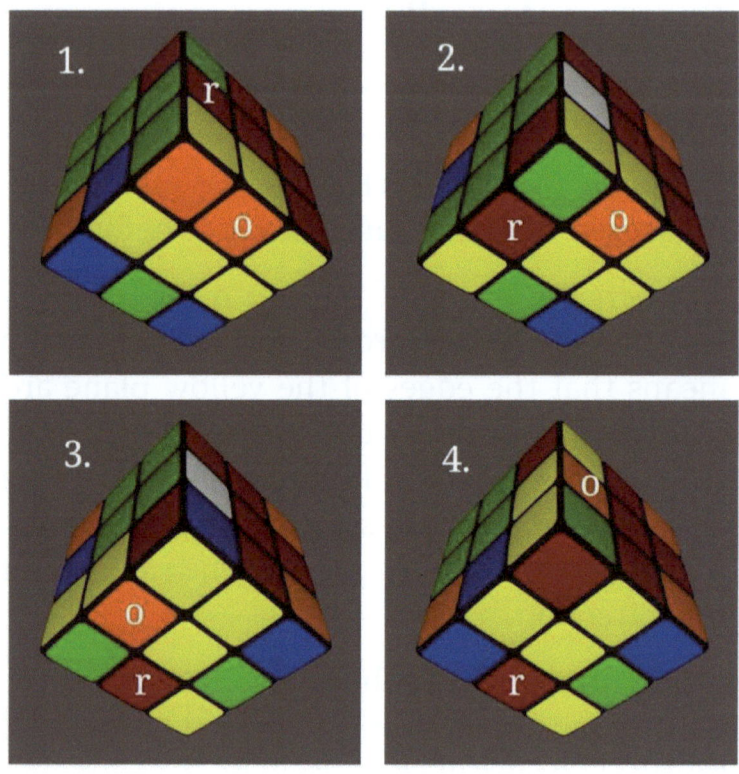

Figure 8. Creating the yellow cross, part 1.

Figure 9. Creating the yellow cross, part 2.

Figure 10. Creating the yellow cross, part 3.

If all edges of the yellow cross are correctly placed we do not need to do anything more. In most cases only two (but never less than two) are correctly placed. If there are only two correctly placed edge pieces on the bottom layer we pick one of the incorrectly placed edge pieces. Let's call it edge-piece A. We turn the bottom layer in order to bring the edge piece A into correct position (not worrying about what happens to other edges on this stage).

We then turn the whole cube so that the edge-piece A is on the location shown by the white circle (on the left-hand side). After that we do the transition depicted by the white arrow of the figure 5 (i.e. do the moves r'DR). This brings the non-yellow side of the edge piece on the spot marked with white circle. Finally we bring the now misplaced edge-piece (let's call it B) to the location where the edge piece A was in the beginning. Finally we bring the edge piece B to it's correct location on one of the side edges by doing the transition marked with white arrow (moves r'DR).

After repeating this one or two times we will have all edge pieces of the whole cube correctly placed and oriented. An example of this stage is given in figure 11. You can understand this as moving one bottom layer edge piece temporarily to the middle layer in order to let another bottom layer edge piece pass by. It is like moving one tram to a side-track in order to let another tram pass and then returning the first tram to the initial track.

The conclusion is then that it is possible to solve all edges without using any algorithms that one needs to memorize. After first forming the white cross we just repeat the same basic transitions several times. You can understand this process and do not need any long and hard-to-memorize algorithms. If you wish you can obviously call the series of three moves (r'DR and its mirroring moves Ld'l') algorithms.

Placing all edges correctly is thus possible by repeating one or two (depending on if the mirroring series are seen as one or two) simple series of three moves. You just bring the piece to a spot shown in figure 5 (white or black depending on case) and do the moves. You obviously will need to figure out case by case which piece shall be moved next and where. After you have decided that by examining the cube it is easy to do the moves.

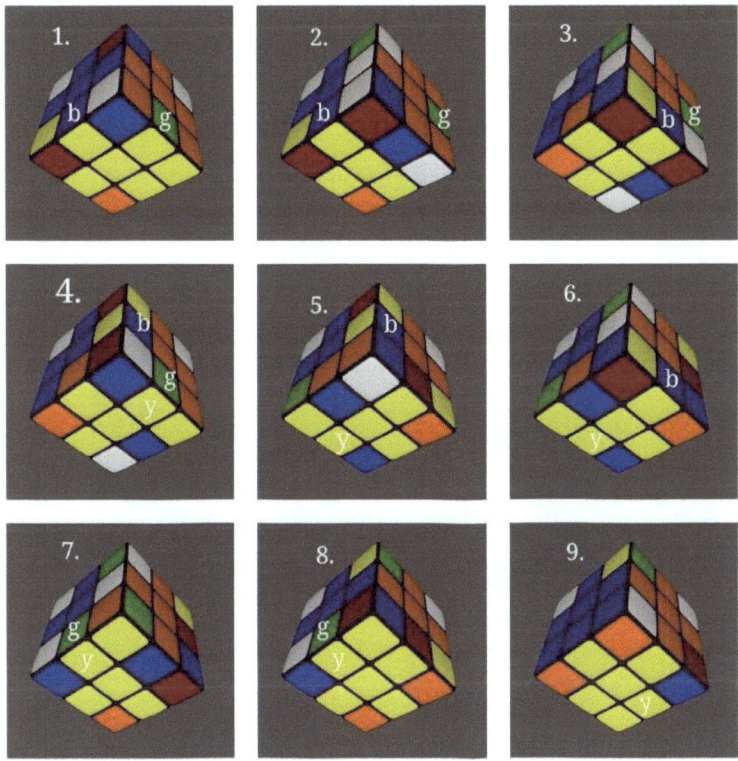

Figure 11. Putting the pieces of the yellow cross into correct order.

Placing the corners

We have now all edges placed and oriented correctly by utilizing just one elementary series of three moves. The cube could at this stage resemble that of the figure 12.

Figure 12. The cube after solving all the edges.

The next step is to place the corners without messing the edges. That can be done by applying several times an elementary series of just four moves (r'd'RD).

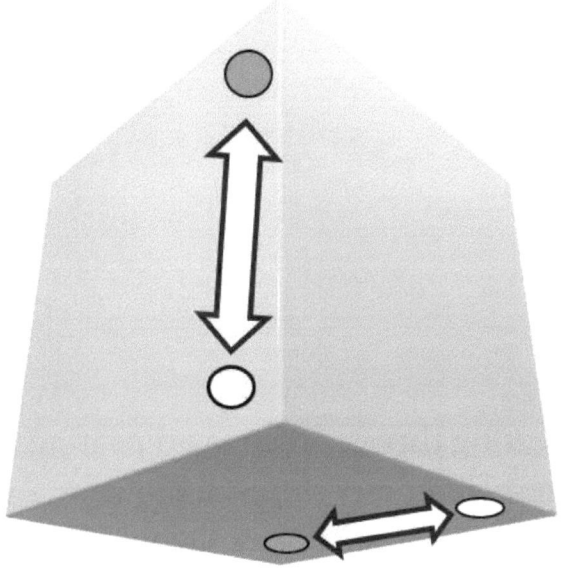

Figure 13. Swapping two corners at a time by repeating three times the elementary series of moves r'd'RD.

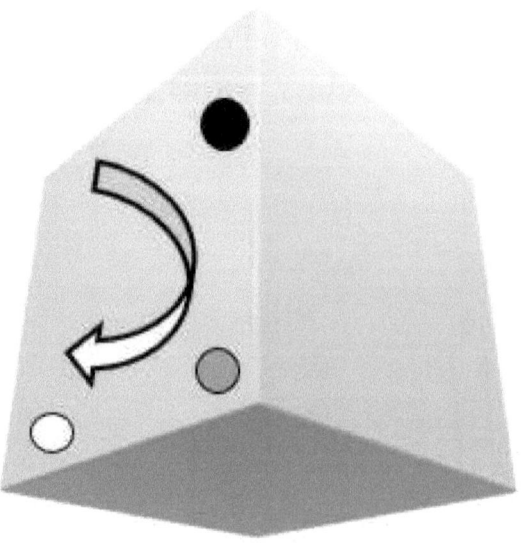

Figure 14. Rotating three corners by repeating three times the elementary series of moves r'd'RD, turning the front plane, doing r'd'RD again three times and finally turning the front plane back to its initial position. The transitions on the back-plane have cancelled out each other.

There are different possibilities to do the corner piece rotations. One is to do successive rotations in order to place all corners of the white plane correctly. It does not matter in which direction the stickers are pointing at this stage, as long as the same three colours are found in the corner pieces as there are on the center pieces of the respective three planes.

Figure 15. The top middle corner gives an example of colours matching with those of the center pices.

Once you have the corners of white plane correctly placed you rotate the corners of the yellow plane until they match colourwise with those of the opposite white-plane corners. This means that apart from the white and yellow stickers the two other colours are the same as in the respective side planes.

After that you look carefully at the sides of the cube (orange, green, red and blue) and try to find a pair of corners that have the white or yellow facets symmtrically placed. This means that that a yellow or write sticker in both of them are facing the same or opposite direction.

The figure 16 shows some examples of symmetrical placements while figure 17 illustrates unsymmetrical cases.

After that you pick any pair of two symmetrically placed corners and orient them correctly by repeating r'd'RD as many times as is needed. After orienting one corner you do not turn the whole cube but just the top-layer. Then you orient the other symmetrically placed corner and pause there. Then you finalize the orientation of the two corners by turning the the top-layer in order to make the colours of the sides match as far as it goes.

Then you look for the next pair of symmetrically placed corners with white or yellow in them and repeat the process.

Note that you can pick any face of the cube (any colour) where you spot symmetrically placed white or yellow stickers. Just turn the cube so that the corners to be oriented are on the top-left and top-right corners of the front face.

Finally you will have two layers solved while there remains only one layer that contains incorrectly oriented corners. After you have reached this point you do not need to worry about symmetrical or unsymmetrical orientations of corners: You simply orient all the corners (1 to 4 pieces) that need to be oriented. After doing this you have solved the whole cube. Congratulations!

Figure 16. Examples of symmetrically placed corners with white or yellow in them. You should start the orientation on pairs of corners like these.

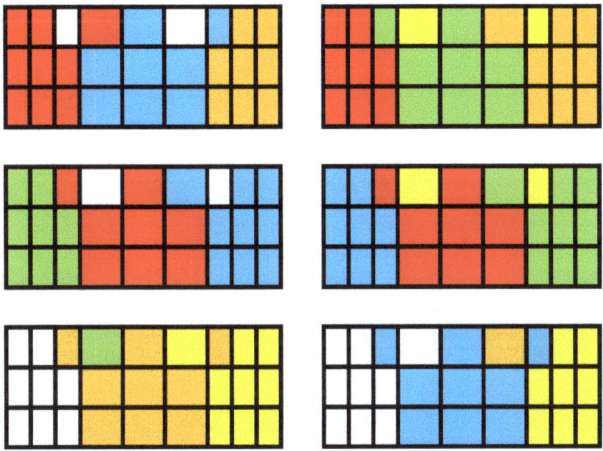

Figure 17. Examples of unsymmetrically placed corners with white or yellow in them. You should not start the orientation on these casew unless it is the last unsolved layer (in that case symmetry is not required any more).

There is, however, one special case, that can occur sometimes: You may enter into a situation where you have just two unoriented corners left but they are not located symmetrically and not even on the same layer but on opposite corners of the cube. This will not be a catastrophic situation because there is a simple trick: You turn any layer by 180 degrees (really any of the six possibilities!). This will bring the last two unoriented corners into symmetrical positions to each other as illustrated in the figure 19. Then you just do the same moves of orientation as explained previously. This sounds almost criminal but it works.

Figure 19. If the last two unoriented corners happen to be opposite yo can turn any of the six layers in order to bring the white or yellow stickers into a symmetry. Then you orient the corners in the way explained before.

After you have oriented the last of these two corners you will be able to complete the solution as illustrated in the figure 20.

Figure 20. Completing the solution with two intuitively obvious moves, after orienting the last opposite corners as shown in the figure 19.

Summary of the solving method

1) Creating the white cross (simple thing).
2) Placing and orienting the edges: Repeat moves r'DR (and/or its mirroring moves Ld'r')
3) Placing and orienting the corners: Repeat moves r'd'RD.

It is not hard to memorize these two simple series of moves and you can even understand how they work. Good luck!